Open Mouth
A Playful Trilogy

Open Mouth
A Playful Trilogy

by

Stephen Erdle

DORRANCE PUBLISHING CO., INC.
PITTSBURGH, PENNSYLVANIA 15222

ISBN # 0-8059-6119-4
Printed in the United States of America

First Printing

For information or to order additional books, please write:
Dorrance Publishing Co., Inc.
701 Smithfield Street
Third Floor
Pittsburgh, Pennsylvania 15222 U.S.A.
1-800-788-7654
Or visit our web site and on-line catalog at
www.dorrancepublishing.com

TO EveryONE

Contents

Stage 1

OUR FIVE FACES
An Emotional Play in One Scene

The setting is a room with a large armchair and a fire. The only character is The Little Person, who sits in the chair. She or he speaks in an Irish accent and is dressed green. Over the fireplace hang the five pictures of the faces, which are depicted below:

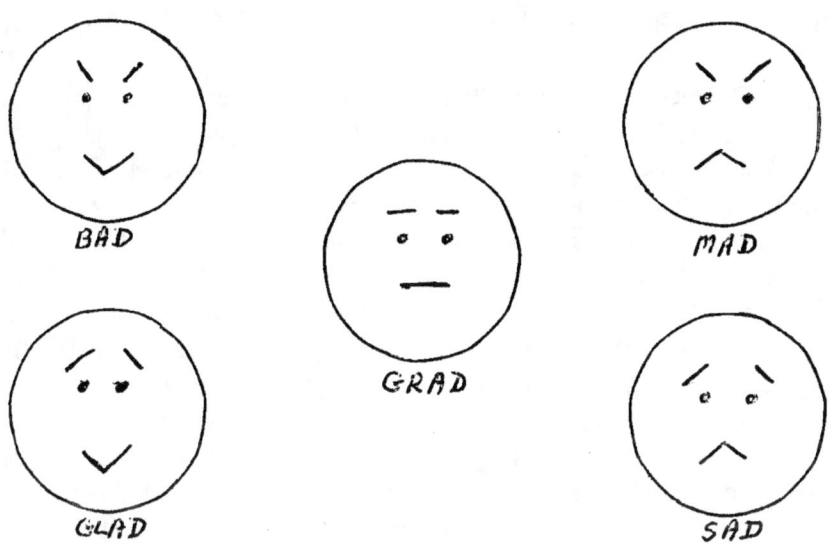

The Little Person Begins

How are you all doing today? Let me introduce myself. I am the last of the little people, don't you know. We little people have lived a long-time, perhaps too long. In any case, I am here to tell you a few things about yourself. You need to know about your five faces. We all have five faces, don't you know.

The five faces are biological in nature. Which of the five faces we feel like at any given time depends upon the state of our nervous system. Experience affects our nervous system. Consistent sensations of good or bad create the five faces.

When we feel BAD, we expect many good sensations and few bad ones. We will be impulsive and carefree. We are reckless. When we are feeling BAD, we think that we can do anything. We have high self-esteem.

When we feel MAD, we expect many good sensations and many bad ones. We will be impulsive and worried. We are aggressive. When we are feeling MAD, we think we should do everything. We have high achievement motivation.

When we feel SAD, we expect few good sensations and many bad ones. We will be reflective and worried. We are defensive. When we are feeling SAD, we think we cannot do anything. We have low self-esteem.

When we feel GLAD, we expect few good sensations and few bad ones. We will be reflective and careless. We are apathetic. When we are feeling Glad, we think we should do nothing. We have low achievement motivation.

But when we feel like a GRAD, we expect moderation in good and bad sensations. We will be intelligent and harmonious. We are purposeful. When we are feeling like a GRAD, we think we should act with moderation. We have moderate self-esteem and achievement motivation.

Now it is important to realize that the five faces can be recreated at any time. However, there is a typical sequence of development of the faces. Most parents protect their children from bad sensations and try to provide them with good sensations. Most parents spoil their children, so most children feel BAD. When we are children, most of us are reckless. When we are teenagers, most of us are no longer protected from bad sensations, so we feel MAD and competitive. We are aggressive. Most of us stay MAD the rest of our lives. When we are in our twenties, a few of us have succeeded and feel BAD again, but most of us continue competing and feel MAD, hoping to someday succeed and feel BAD. Some of us have given up the fight and feel SAD. We are defensive. In our thirties, some of us who feel SAD either turn to alcohol to feel GLAD (but wake up SAD again in the morning), or turn to philosophy and religion to feel GLAD. We are apathetic. When we are in our forties, some us who have turned to philosophy and religion realize that the majority of people are still BAD, MAD, or SAD and we want to change things but we don't know how. So we become MAD again. Along the way, however, some of us learn the nature of our five faces and how to manage them. We have become GRADS and can teach others how to understand their faces, don't you know.

Now, there are three ways to manage the five faces. Experience can change our faces. Changing levels of chemicals in the nervous system through drugs or breathing exercises are the two temporary ways to change our faces. Reforming our expectations is slower, but the most lasting way to change faces.

Drugs can re-create our faces. There are four common recreational drugs used to control our faces, and anybody can acquire them. Alcohol decreases worry (making us BAD or GLAD), while nicotine increases worry (making us MAD or SAD). Marijuana decreases impulsiveness (making us GLAD or SAD) while caffeine increases impulsiveness (making us BAD or MAD). There are also many prescription drugs used to control our faces. The problems with ingesting chemicals is that they can have negative side effects, and they are expensive. But they work, so many people use them.

Now, breathing exercises can re-create our faces less expensively (physically and economically) than drugs, by altering levels of oxygen and carbon dioxide in the bloodstream. Long in-breaths and long out-breaths (slow breathing) decrease worry, while short in-breaths and short out-breaths increase worry. Short in-breaths and long out-breaths decrease impulsiveness, while long in-breaths and short out-breaths increase impulsiveness. Breathing exercises work, and have been used by yoga practitioners for thousands of years. Breathing exercises can be combined to create any of the five faces.

But reforming our expectations can change our faces in a more lasting fashion. When we are children most of us expect to be the richest, best, and the most famous. When we mature, we recognize that those expectations were unrealistic. Lowering one's expectations of bad sensations will decrease worry, while raising expectations of bad sensations will increase worry. Lowing expectations of good sensation decreases impulsiveness while raising expectations of good sensations will increase impulsiveness. Reforming expectations also can be combined to create any of the five faces.

The most lasting way to reform our expectations is to reform society. When we feel wealthy, we expect many good sensations and few bad ones, so we feel BAD. Our political affiliation is often conservative. When we feel overworked, we expect many good sensations and many bad ones, so we feel MAD, and we may align ourselves politically with labor unions. When we feel impoverished, we expect few good sensations and many bad ones, so we feel SAD. Our political affiliation is often Socialist or Communist. When we feel that we should reject materialism, we expect few good sensations and few bad ones, so we feel GLAD, and our political affiliation is often Anarchist. When we feel educated, however, we expect moderation in good and bad sensations, so we feel like grads, and we will likely adopt a humanist political stance.

The minority of people, those who feel BAD (the wealthy), often deceive the majority of people, those who feel MAD (the overworked), to make them feel GLAD (philosophical) and keep them from feeling SAD (impoverished). The BAD have told the MAD, and the SAD, the GLAD, and the GRAD to cherish freedom, so that the MAD will support the BAD in the hope that they too someday will feel BAD and join the elite.

The GRAD, however, have asked the BAD, the MAD, the SAD, and the GLAD to seek justice (freedom from injustice, not freedom to be unjust), so that all people can learn to feel like GRADS while they are at work and feel GLAD when they are at play. When we all learn to manage our faces, all people, big and little alike, will be GLAD more often, don't you know.

Curtain

Stage 2

DECONSTRUCTING HAIRY PETER
A Thoughtful Play in One Scene

The setting is a lecture hall with a lectern. The only character is The Professor, who stands at the lectern. She or he speaks in an Austrian accent, and is dressed in black.

The Professor begins.

Good day, everyone, My name is Professor Always Mumblemore and I have a fascinating story to tell you. The story completely confirms my new theory of postmodern sexual analysis. It is the case of Little Hairy Peter.

The boy was emotionally scarred by the death of his parents, from AIDS in the 1980s. Fortunately, he was born free of the virus. He was a boy who lived.

When Hairy Peter was ten years old, his sexual dreams began. Hairy's first dream was that he was at a zoo and a sleeping snake rose up and winked at him. The snake said that it had been confined all its life and wanted to go into the forest where it belonged. So Hairy let the snake loose.

The symbolic content of the dream shows the awakening sexuality of a young boy. The boy's penis (the snake) had begun stirring and wanted to enter a vagina (the forest). The boy yearned to let nature take its course.

Hairy's second dream was that he was receiving letters trying to tell him something, but that he was unable to read them. Hairy dreamt that a large haggard man finally told him that the evil FullofDeath had killed his parents. The haggard man also pulled a shabby pink umbrella from his trousers, but not being entirely proficient with it, used it to cause a pain in the backside of a young boy. Then he invited young Hairy away to a magical school.

This dream too has obvious symbolic content. The boy has discovered the connection between sex and his parents' death. A sexually mature man informed him that his parents died from the dark side of sex (AIDS) and that he can learn about his sexuality from books when he goes to secondary school. The boy also has learned that homosexual behavior, especially anal sex, is linked to AIDS.

Hairy's third dream was that the haggard man took him to a hidden alley that displays magical things. Hairy found his wand there. It was eleven inches long, bigger than most others were. He also met Professor QueerAll from his new school, who was effeminate, and many other men and women who found him attractive.

Symbolically, the boy fantasized about entering a street of sex shops. He perhaps had been in one once with an older friend and seen pictures of naked people that caused him to have an erection (the wand). He also seems to have been aware that he had sexual appeal to some men. Both men and women in the sex alley tried to seduce him.

Hairy's fourth and most detailed dream was that he was at a magical school. One of his teachers was Professor Snake, who made potions, and he met a girl his age, Hermaphrodite. Hairy made his broomstick rise at his first attempt, but Hermaphrodite could not. She first rejected him, but when he saved her from a dirty troll in the girl's washroom, she accepted him. Then he became a school hero for being one of the youngest boys at school to catch the Golden Snatch. Hairy first suspected Professor Snake of evil. He then entered a trapdoor into a tunnel. Inside the tunnel, however, he found that it was Professor QueerAll who was the bad one. Professor QueerAll had traveled too much and had come in contact with the evil FullofDeath. He tried to cover his sickness with a turban but Hairy finally realized that FullofDeath had infected Professor QueeerAll. He killed Professor QueerAll but the evil FullofDeath escaped.

Professor Snake symbolizes the penis, obviously. The potions he creates are the fluids that come from the penis, urine and semen. It at first seemed evil. The girl, Hermaphrodite, represents the boy's awareness that girls are not entirely different from boys. Boys, however, have the natural ability to create erections (the rising broomstick) while girls need practice in the art. When he saves the girl from a pedophile, she accepts him and he enjoys his first sexual experience (catching the Golden Snatch). The boy realizes, after he has lost his virginity (entering the trap door into the tunnel), that the penis (Professor Snake) is not bad. He has learned that AIDS (FullofDeath) first infected promiscuous homosexual men (Professor QueerAll), and that condoms (the turban) are used by infected people to continue having sex. However, the boy also recognizes that reacting against homosexuals will not eradicate the virus. The boy has reached maturity in the postmodern sexual world.

Curtain

Stage 3

On-Us

An Active Play in One Scene

The setting is a courtroom. At the front is an empty chair. The Public Defender is the only character, and stands to the side of the chair dressed in white. She or he addresses the audience in a Southern American accent.

Mighty fine day-to-day, isn't it?

You all are members of a jury. We all are, really—all the time. Today, however, we shall be asked to vote. We shall be asked to judge guilty or not guilty in the trial of the millennia. We shall be asked to distinguish right from wrong. Today is judgment day. The onus is on us.

I am standing before you, a simple public defender, appointed by the court. I have been asked to present the closing argument in this case. Opposing me is a formidable team of prosecutors and witnesses for the prosecution.

The prosecution has presented testimony for over five millennia. The prosecution has filled libraries with testimony. The prosecution has tried to confuse you with complexity. Now, the prosecution has run out of witnesses.

I shall present the case for the defense in less than one hour. When we examine the evidence and the testimony, it turns out that all is quite simple, really.

From the testimony we have learned that two rivals gangs back the prosecution. They have tried to be secretive but we know who they are. They have promised the prosecutors and you, the jury, possible riches and immortality if they win the case. But are they telling you the truth?

One gang is Physics, alias "Natural Philosophy," alias "Science." Now, they control the West Side of Town.

Ontology, alias "Knowledge of Nature." leads Physics, but Epistemology, alias "Nature of Knowledge," has been shown to be aligned with Ontology.

The other gang is Ethics, alias "Moral Philosophy," alias "Religion." Now, they control the Middle East and the East sides of Town. Politics, alias "Art of Society," leads Ethics, but Aesthetics, alias "Society of Art," has growing influence.

Both gangs, however, despite their differences, have accused a mysterious figure they call Metaphysics, alias "the Supernatural," alias "The Mystic," of controlling the whole Town, including Physics and Ethics, and ultimately, being responsible for the crime of the millennia: human suffering.

But what have we before us here, today? I see only an empty chair. Neither Physics nor Ethics has been able to produce this mysterious Metaphysics.

Now, I am simple-minded. I doubt, therefore I am—a public defender.

I shall show that there is reasonable doubt that Metaphysics is responsible for human suffering.

I shall show that there is reasonable doubt that Metaphysics even exists.

In fact, though it is not at all my job, I shall show that all the evidence is consistent with the conclusion that Physics is responsible for originating human suffering and Ethics is responsible for perpetuating it.

We all heard the testimony of the witness, Aristotle. The people in Town, and I quote, "by nature, want to know." And why do they want to know? They want to know for good. Remember the testimony of the witness, Hammurabi. I quote what he had engraved in stone over four millennia ago: "Enlighten the land and further the welfare of the people."

So, let us review the case. What is the testimony?

Epistemology, alias "Nature of Knowledge," testified first. Epistemology initially testified that knowledge was due entirely to Metaphysics and was not connected to Physics at all. Epistemology brought out expert witnesses to testify.

Plato testified that there was a duality between the body and the soul. We heard that the body was due to Physics but that the soul (the source of knowledge) was due to Metaphysics and influenced the physical. Descartes, obviously intimidated by Politics, testified that the soul was in the pineal gland in the brain. Body—Soul—BS.

The witness Freud admitted that the brain was an electrochemical machine. There is no duality. We learned that knowledge is physical, not metaphysical at all.

Under cross-examination, Epistemology finally admitted that right and wrong are probably decisions generated by the activity of the nervous systems of animals.

We learned that animals need to distinguish right and wrong to avoid bad sensations and approach good sensations. We learned that right and wrong are probabilistic and subjective (both individually and collectively).

Epistemology admitted that the modern computing machine's electrical system is patterned after the nervous system's electrochemical system. Sensory, or afferent, neurons of the peripheral nervous system receive input; association (or what might be called perceptual) neurons of the central nervous system process information; and motor, or efferent neurons, of the peripheral nervous system execute output.

We learned that sensations produce perceptions, which produce actions, which produce new sensations.

Epistemology admitted that perceptions are probably right or wrong. We learned that consistency of perceptions is the basis for perceptual verification (learning, memory, and scientific or legal proof). Some stories are more believable than other stories. Stories that are consistent with evidence are more likely to be right than stories inconsistent with evidence. We try to minimize the probability of being wrong and maximize the probability of being right. We heard that right and wrong are beyond a reasonable doubt. They are neither absolute nor are they arbitrary.

We learned that animals decide whether sensations, and the actions which produce them, are probably right or wrong. We call sensations and actions good or bad, and call it feeling. Feeling is activity of the peripheral nervous system.

We also must decide whether the perceptions are probably right or wring. We call perceptions true or false, and call it thinking. Thinking is activity of the central nervous system.

In the end, Epistemology admitted that we feel sensations (probably good or bad), think about them (probably true or false), and act accordingly (approach or avoid).

After the testimony of Epistemology, we began to have reasonable doubt that Metaphysics is responsible for human suffering. Epistemology reluctantly admitted that Metaphysics plays no role in the nature of knowledge. Knowledge comes from input to the central nervous system. The input is initiated by the physical world. Epistemology admitted allegiance with Ontology—and Physics.

That brings us to the testimony of the leader of the gang of Physics, Ontology, alias "Knowledge of Nature."

First, Ontology maintained that it had no connection to Physics but instead worked directly for the mysterious Metaphysics.

The witness Plato testified that there was a duality between the real and the ideal.

But the story was inconsistent. We heard the witness Aristotle testify that there was no duality.

Aristotle, in fact, shocked the courtroom when he testified that there was no Metaphysics at all, only Physics and Ethics—the actual and the potential—what is and what could be. The whole story was staring to unfold.

Recall that Ontology's first testimony was that Metaphysics created everything in seven days.

Under cross-examination, however, Ontology testified that Metaphysics created a big bang that produced forces that move matter-energy in space-time. But was Ontology telling the probable truth?

Remember Epistemology's initial testimony. The soul causes action. Force causes motion. Eventually, however, Epistemology admitted that motion causes force. Sensation causes perception, which causes action. Sensation is produced by physical motion.

Perhaps matter-energy moves with space-time, always producing forces. I am only speculating, of course.

But remember the cross-examination of the witnesses.

Heraclitus testified that all was flux. The Buddha agreed.

Hume testified that mathematics was tautological (circular). Numbers name perceptions, he admitted. Remember Exhibit A of the Defense. Was it two faces or one vase? Does two equal one? The Pythagoreans were visibly shaken as they listened to the testimony.

Aristotle testified that there must be a simple body that revolves naturally, and no void.

Descartes testified that there were three dimensions, fundamental rotations, and no empty space.

The particle physicists testified that all was composed of gluons, fundamental particles that are constantly moving and have eight states.

The quantum physicists testified that all was discontinuous motion.

Einstein testified that matter and energy are equivalent through motion. $E=MC^2$. Einstein also corroborated Aristotle's and Descartes's testimony that there was no void, no empty space-time. Einstein testified that matter-energy is spacio-temporally extended.

The courtroom was silent when Physics admitted that, in 1965, the void was falsified when background microwave radiation was observed. The witness Popper assured us that if evidence is inconsistent with a theory, then the theory is falsified, corroborating the testimony of Epistemology.

The witnesses Aristotle, Decartes, and Einstein were probably right. There is no void. _Nihil non est_—nothing is not.

Ontology continued to insist that the universe was expanding, despite the evidence that there was nothing to expand into. Ontology testified that there was a frequency shift of light from distant starts. If the stars were expanding, there would be such a frequency shift.

Now, you will remember that is when I called Epistemology back to the stand.

Under cross-examination, Epistemology admitted that Ontology's argument was logically flawed. We learned that Ontology was confirming the consequent. Perhaps there was another cause for frequency shifts. Perhaps rotation causes frequency shifts.

What is the probable truth, then, about the movements of Ontology?

Now, I am a simple public defender. But I can multiply two by two by two and get eight.

It may well be that matter-energy has always moved with space-time and produces forces (and frequency shifts) through the interactions of three-dimensional, revolving, intersecting, fundamental motions.

I ask you, would not clockwise or counter-clockwise rotation on three independent dimensions result in eight relative states? Two times two times two. Gluons, perhaps.

I ask you, would not rotation on one axis of a fundamental motion continuously reverse when rotation occurred on either of the other two axes? Quantum fluctuation, perhaps.

I ask you, would not adjacent motions with similar rotation parallel axes be mutually inhibitory? Matter gravitating together, perhaps.

And finally, I ask you, would not adjacent motions with dissimilar rotations on parallel axes be mutually exciting? Energy radiating apart, perhaps.

Ontology's plan is apparent for all to see. Ontology never stops moving but now we know Ontology's movements. Ontology is constantly creating revolution.

We must recognize that Physics alone may be responsible for human suffering. Perhaps, Ontology, through revolution, originated human suffering and Epistemology recognized it. There is no evidence that Metaphysics played any role at all.

We now turn our attention to the testimony of the other half of the prosecution: Ethics.

I shall show that Ethics is a simple follower, and is only responsible for perpetuating human suffering, not originating it.

Before examining the testimony of Aesthetics, alias "Society of Art," we shall review the testimony of Politics, alias "Art of Society," the leader of Ethics.

We remember Politics' first testimony. Politics also disavowed any connection with Physics and testified to have worked directly for Metaphysics. The witness Moses testified that the law was given to him personally by Metaphysics. The witnesses Jesus and Mohammed agreed.

Lao Tsu, Confucius, and the Buddha, however, stunned the courtroom when they testified that all, including Ethics, was entirely physical. We learned that Religion without Metaphysics was possible.

Politics finally confessed the probable truth. Politics testified that it followed Physics, principally Ontology.

Politics admitted that it changed its testimony from divine leadership to national representative democracy because of the influence of Ontology. When asked why there was not global justice, why there was not one law (democratically determined), why there was not one currency and fair trade, Politics looked helplessly at Ontology for support for pluralism or at least dualism (them and us), but Ontology looked away. Why? Perhaps there is no duality. Epistemology testified that we are one—they are we. We do to ourselves what we do to others. Epistemology testified that people want justice: freedom from injustice, not freedom to be unjust.

Finally, Politics admitted that global justice was possible. Politics confessed that it had blindly followed Ontology and was unknowingly perpetuating human suffering.

Now, what is the role of Aesthetics, alias "Society of Art," in this sorry tale of revolution and human suffering? Aesthetics, too, is a simple follower. Aesthetics has repeatedly turned to Politics for support in influencing Ethics.

We have seen and heard Aesthetics tell many stories, paint many pictures, sing many songs, and dance many dances.

Aesthetics first swore allegiance to Metaphysics, testifying to an absolute and divine truth and beauty. Then, following Ontology we heard Aesthetics change its testimony to assert that anything was possible. Aesthetics testified that it thought that the logical consequence was that anything could be right or wrong.

Aesthetics is not always logical though, is it? Under cross-examination, Aesthetics was forced to admit that just because Ontology testified that anything is possible, does not mean that everything is equally likely or equally right and wrong. Remember Epistemology's testimony. Right and wrong are beyond a reasonable doubt. Aesthetics, finally abandoning Ontology, agreed with Epistemology. Aesthetics admitted that the People in Town want to know what is probably right and wrong, not what is possibly right and wrong.

So, what have we learned in this courtroom today? We have learned that there is reasonable doubt that the mysterious Metaphysics plays any role in originating or perpetuating human suffering. In fact, we have learned that there is reasonable doubt that Metaphysics exists at all. Epistemology taught us that if the evidence does not fit, then we must acquit.

I hope you all will agree with me that we must vote not guilty in the trial of the millennia. Ironically, we must vote in defense of Metaphysics.

Before you vote, however, let me remind you that we are here today only to determine the possible role Metaphysics in human suffering, not to determine the actual cause of human suffering.

It is obvious that we need another trial, in which Physics and Ethics can be accused directly of the crime of human suffering. I have offered only speculation here today.

If, however, Physics and Ethics, in a court of law, are shown, beyond a reasonable doubt, to be responsible for the crime of human suffering, I recommend leniency for Epistemology, Politics, and Aesthetics.

Epistemology has agreed to inform the people of the movements of Ontology, and lead Physics.

Ontology will keep on creating revolution. Revolution is natural for Ontology. Remember Ontology's smirk when saying, "I'll change." I'll bet Ontology will change, and keep on changing, forever.

Ethics, both Politics and Aesthetics, however, are beginning to recognize that they have been unknowingly perpetuating human suffering and vow to work to alleviate human suffering in the future.

So, I recommend community service for Epistemology and Ethics. We must work with, not against change—Ontology. The People in Town must recognize Physics and Ethics and abandon faith in Metaphysics. We must reject visions of riches and immortality and content ourselves with justice and humanity.

I think we may have learned a valuable lesson in this courtroom today. I think we may have learned the social implications of the probable rotationally kinetic nature of quantum gravitation and radiation.

Things change.

Curtain

www.ingramcontent.com/pod-product-compliance
Lightning Source LLC
Chambersburg PA
CBHW060351290526
45791CB00004B/1636